Teachers' notes

Aims of this book

These pages of patterns encourage children to practise the motor control of actions and movements which make up our writing system. This is a useful preparation for practising letter shapes. In order for children to practise the patterns further, they could use tracing paper to go over an already completed page or use coloured pencils to go over pencil marks.

The aims of this book are:

- to develop fine motor control;
- to establish a left-to-right directionality;
- to practise the movements necessary in writing;
- to establish the habit of producing small differences between letter strokes, e.g., i/l;
- to allow children to practise making relaxed and comfortable hand movements before having to concentrate on producing specific letter shapes;
- to give children the opportunity to appreciate the differences between 'on the lines', 'above the lines' and 'below the lines'.

Developing handwriting skills

This book contains a series of activities to help children at the initial stage of developing handwriting. It will also be of use to the older children who are not forming their letters properly. Correct formation of letters helps children to achieve a fast and legible hand. There is often a dilemma for teachers when they notice children writing a letter incorrectly, but they are absorbed in their work. Should they stop the child writing and insist upon the correct letter formation, or should they let them finish their writing? Each situation has to be assessed individually, but, on the whole, it is best not to interrupt children who are concentrating on the message they want to communicate. It is better to wait and then offer
the child learns the c
who have become c
letter formation pose
need to spend time re
opportunity to ensure
the correct movement ... think
about it.

Posture for writing

- Children should be encouraged to sit well back on the chairs in order to gain maximum stability.
- Children should have their feet firmly on the floor. In a writing corner it may be possible to provide a foot rest (telephone directory) for the smaller child.
- Children should not sit hunched over their writing. This is generally caused by the child being too tall for the chair and table provided. In a writing corner a choice of chairs and table heights could be provided.
- Both hands/arms should be resting on the writing surface. The free hand should be used to control the paper.

Writing implements

- As a rule of thumb, the thicker the barrel of the pencil, the easier it is to produce fine motor control. However, if a pencil is too heavy, then obviously this control is lost. If children are experiencing problems with pencil control, a pencil grip may alleviate the problem. There are a variety of these on the market – some even offer moulded grips which take account of the left-handed, as well as the right-handed child (see LDA and Taskmaster).
- Children do need to experiment with as wide a variety of implements as possible, from wax crayons to felt-tipped pens.

Pen holds

Traditionally, children have been taught to hold the pen between the thumb and the first finger, with the second finger acting as a support. Many children adopt this style very quickly. However, an alternative pen hold has been suggested by Rosemary Sassoon where the pencil is held between the index and the middle finger; this can offer a more comfortable hold and greater pencil control (see *Teaching Handwriting* (1990), Stanley Thornes). Care should be taken to prevent children adopting awkward or tense pencil holds, since this will restrict the speed of their writing as they get older.

Paper position

Young children often prefer to have paper placed directly in front of them, but as they become more confident writers, they should be gently persuaded to move the paper either to the right or left of their body and sloping at approximately 30–40 degrees, according to their handedness. There is no exact position, but comfort and movement across the page should determine the final position.

Helping the left-hander

- Sit the left-handed child on a slightly higher chair so that she can see over the top of the piece of work. This also gives more freedom of movement.
- If possible, demonstrate letter formation with your left hand.
- A pencil grip can be helpful as left-handers tend to grip very hard. The pencil grip, by thickening the pencil and preventing the fingers from slipping, does relieve some of the pressure.
- Ensure the child has enough space. He should not be knocking either the wall or a friend.
- Encourage the child to try to hold the pencil farther from the point. This enables the left-hander to see what she has written.
- The paper should be positioned to the left of centre and tilted slightly to the right to give more freedom of movement. Young children often find this rather disturbing, and will need gentle but frequent encouragement.

Main handwriting patterns

There are five main handwriting patterns which will be introduced in handwriting families:

1 r n m h p b

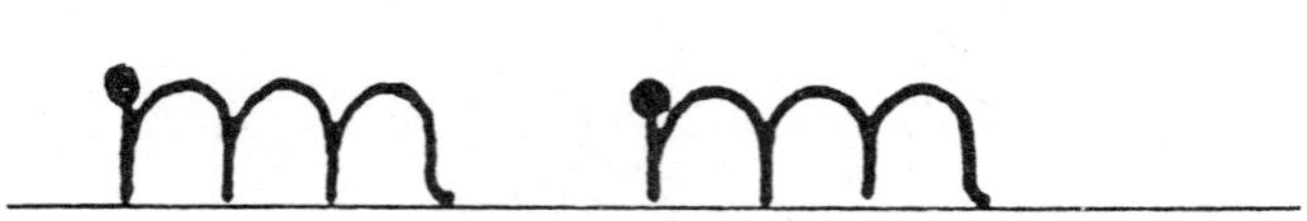

2 i u y l t

3 v w x

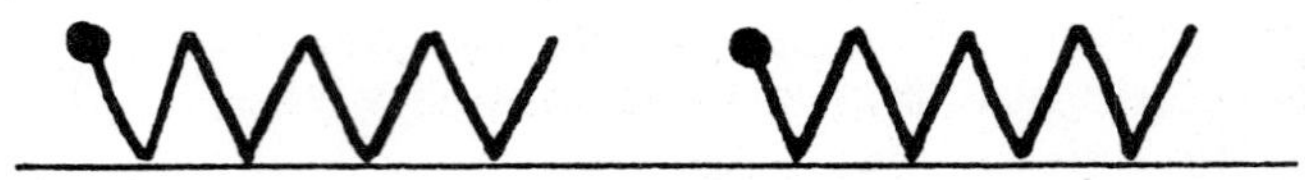

4 i u y l t (reinforcing pattern)

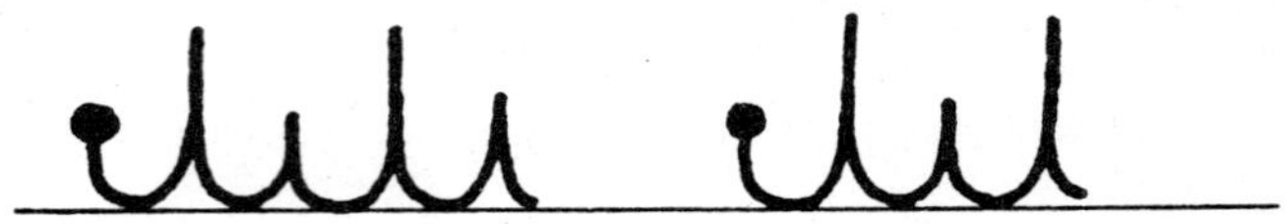

5 a c d e g o q

NB Characters f k j s z are not in a letter family, while some other letters fit into more than one family. It is always worth spending a little time explaining to the children what each activity is trying to achieve in terms of letter formation. Children should not think that handwriting is an easy option, but something which requires hard work and practice, and of which they can be very proud.

Further reading

A Practical Guide to Children's Handwriting, R. Sassoon (1983) Thames and Hudson

The Development of Handwriting Skills: a Resource Book for Teachers, C. Jarman (1979) Basil Blackwell

Handwriting: a New Perspective, R. Sassoon (1990) Stanley Thornes

Teaching Left-handed Children, M. Clark (1974) Hodder and Stoughton

Creating a Handwriting Policy, D. Bentley (1991) University of Reading

Joining the ABC, C. Cripps (1991) LDA

Notes on individual activities

General note: Some children might like to colour the activities using crayons. They should be careful not to obscure the patterns.

Pages 5–6
These two pages introduce to the child the concept of patterns. Encourage him to use the index finger of his writing hand to trace the patterns. This will give him a feel for the rhythm of the pattern and enable the teacher to check on the starting points and left/right sequencing before the child begins with his pencil.

Page 7
This pattern will introduce letters r n m h p b. It is very important that the children start at the dot as this is the starting point. Discuss it with them first, because all letters start at the top, except d and e.

Pages 8–9
These pages offer further reinforcement and practice of the pattern on page 7.

Page 10
This pattern will introduce the following letters: i u y l t.

Pages 11–12
These pages give further reinforcement and practice for the pattern on page 10.

Page 13
This pattern will introduce the letters v w x.

Pages 14–15
These pages offer further reinforcement and practice of the pattern on page 13.

Page 16
This pattern will reinforce the letters i u y l t. The pattern emphasises the ascenders.

Pages 17–18
These pages offer further reinforcement and practice for the pattern on page 16.

Page 19
These patterns will introduce the following letters: a c d e g o q.

Pages 20–21
These pages offer further reinforcement and practice for the pattern on page 19.

Pages 22–23
These pages can be used to check the correct formation of the patterns.

Page 24
Encourage the children to try the patterns by themselves. These can make attractive borders round their work.

Pages 25–30
These pages are for those children whose pencil control needs further reinforcing. The patterns round the edge extend the handwriting patterns.

Pages 31–32
These line guides will provide alternative spacing according to the child's needs and stage of development.

National Curriculum: English

The activities in this book support the following requirements of the PoS for KS1 for the National Curriculum for English:

Writing

- In **handwriting**, pupils should be taught to hold a pencil comfortably in order to develop a legible style that follows the conventions of written English, including:
  - writing from left to right and from top to bottom of the page;
  - starting and finishing letters correctly;
  - regularity of size and shape of letters;
  - regularity of spacing of letters and words.

  They should be taught the conventional ways of forming letters, both lower case and capitals.

Scottish 5-14 Curriculum: English

Attainment outcome	Strand	Attainment target	Level
Writing	Handwriting and presentation	Form letters and space words legibly.	A

See inside back cover for Northern Ireland Curriculum links

Watch points for teachers

- Handwriting patterns link up with joined letters.
- Tracing patterns and letters can help.
- All letters except d and e START AT THE TOP.
- Use capital letters at the beginning of words. DO NOT JOIN.
- Joined letters help spelling.
- Check sitting position. It should be both feet on the floor, forearm on the table.
- Wider-lined paper is a help when you are learning to write – or write on every other line.
- Encourage children not to hold the pencil close to the point.
- Triangular pencils provide a comfortable pencil grip.
- Give lots of praise for effort.
- If the children like unlined paper, use a line guide.

● **Name** ______________________________

● Follow the pattern with your pencil. Start at the dot.
Practise the pattern in the spaces.

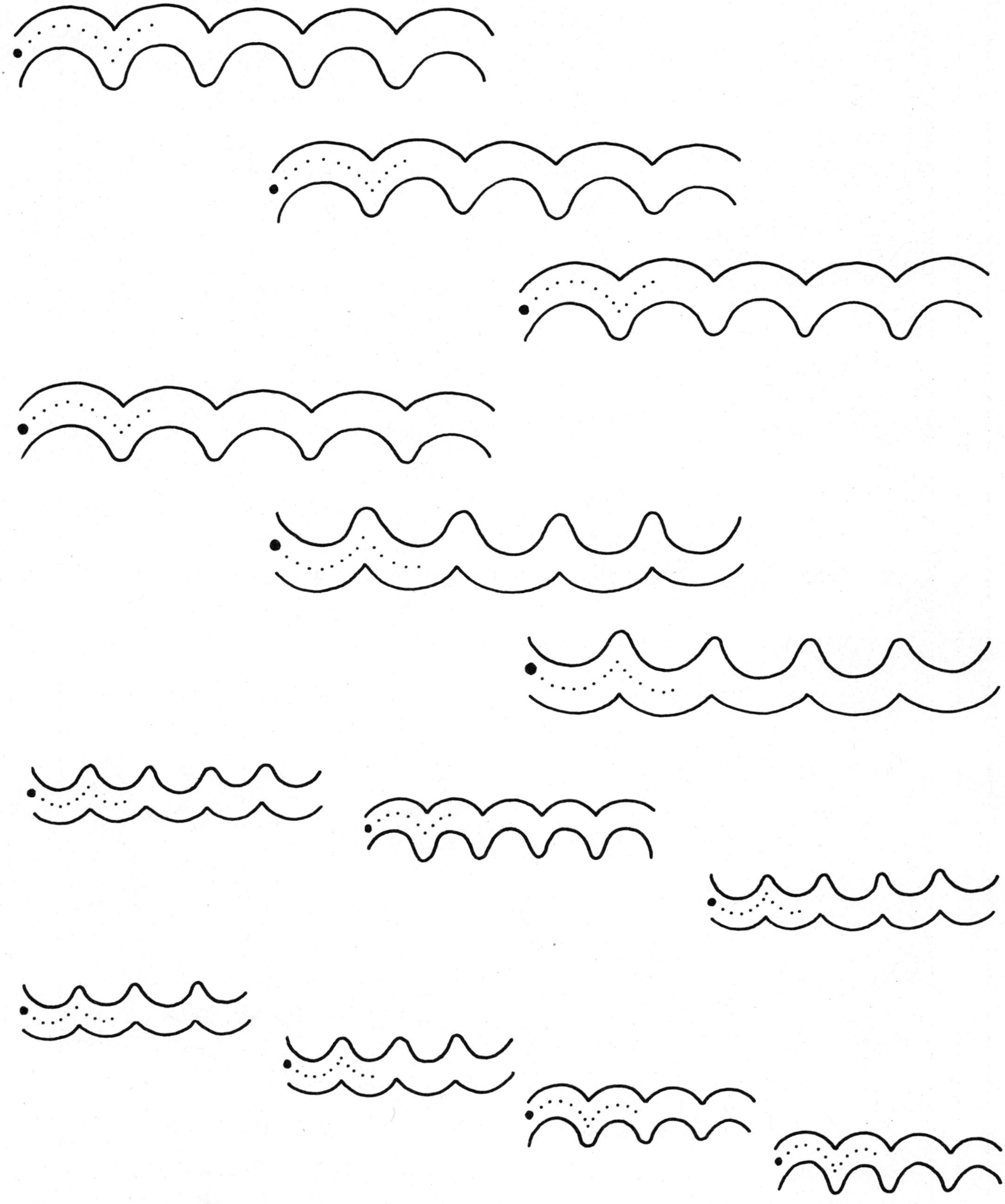

● Try some patterns yourself.

● **Name** ______________________________

● Follow the pattern with your pencil. Start at the dot.

● Try some patterns yourself.

● **Name** ______________________

● Go over the pattern and copy in between. Remember – start at the dot!

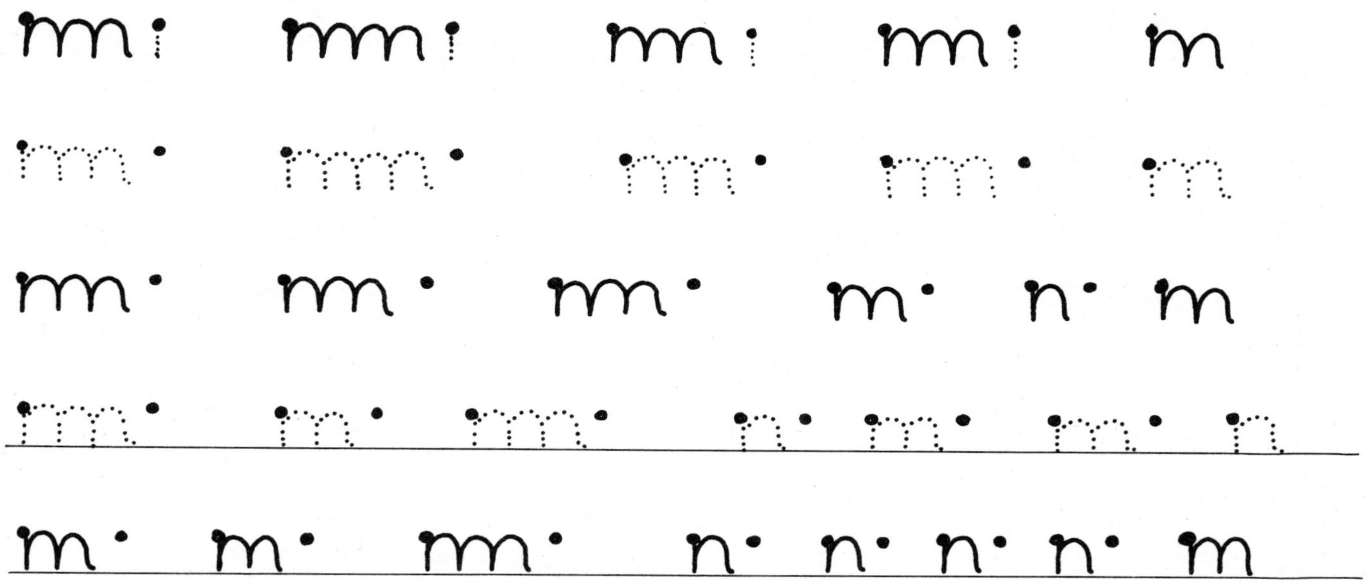

● Finish the line. m n

● Finish the patterns on the fish.

Name ______________________________

- Finish the patterns round the flowers.

- Finish the pattern on the roof.

- Finish the patterns on the tortoises.

● Name ____________________

● Draw the patterns on the sheep and the birds.

● **Name** ______________________

● Go over the pattern and copy in between. Remember – start at the dot!

● Finish the line. u u u u

● Finish the patterns on the clowns.

● Name ______________________

● Finish the patterns on the caterpillars.

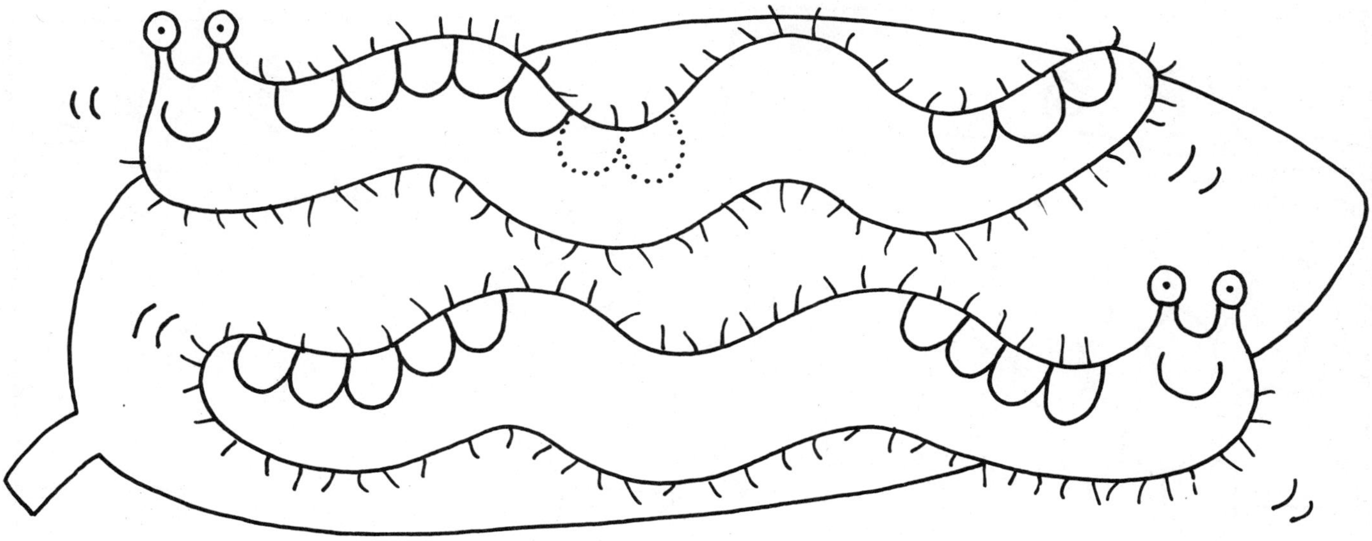

● Finish the patterns on the shells.

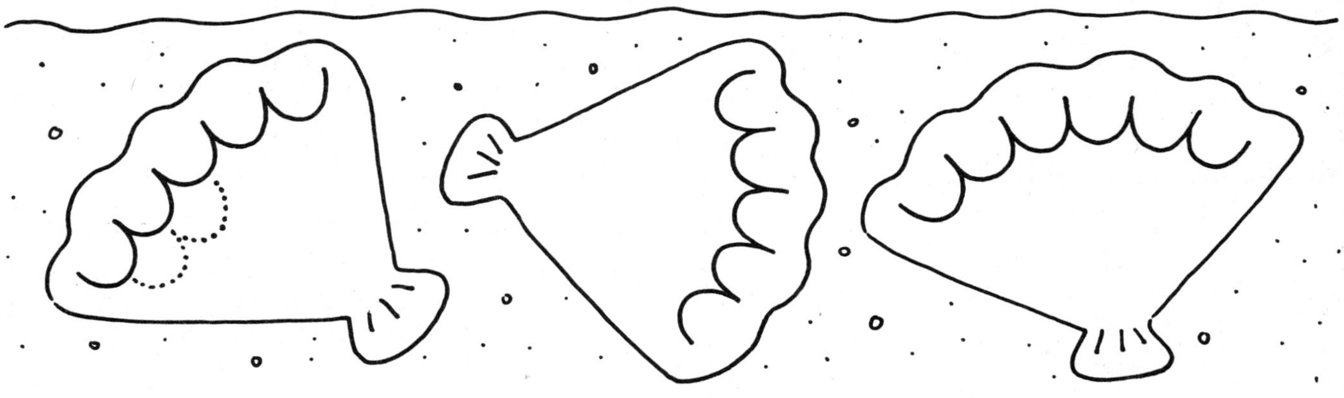

● Finish the patterns on the trees.

● **Name** ______________________

● Draw the patterns on the grapes and the flowers.

● **Name** ______________________________

● Go over the pattern and copy in between. Remember – start at the dot!

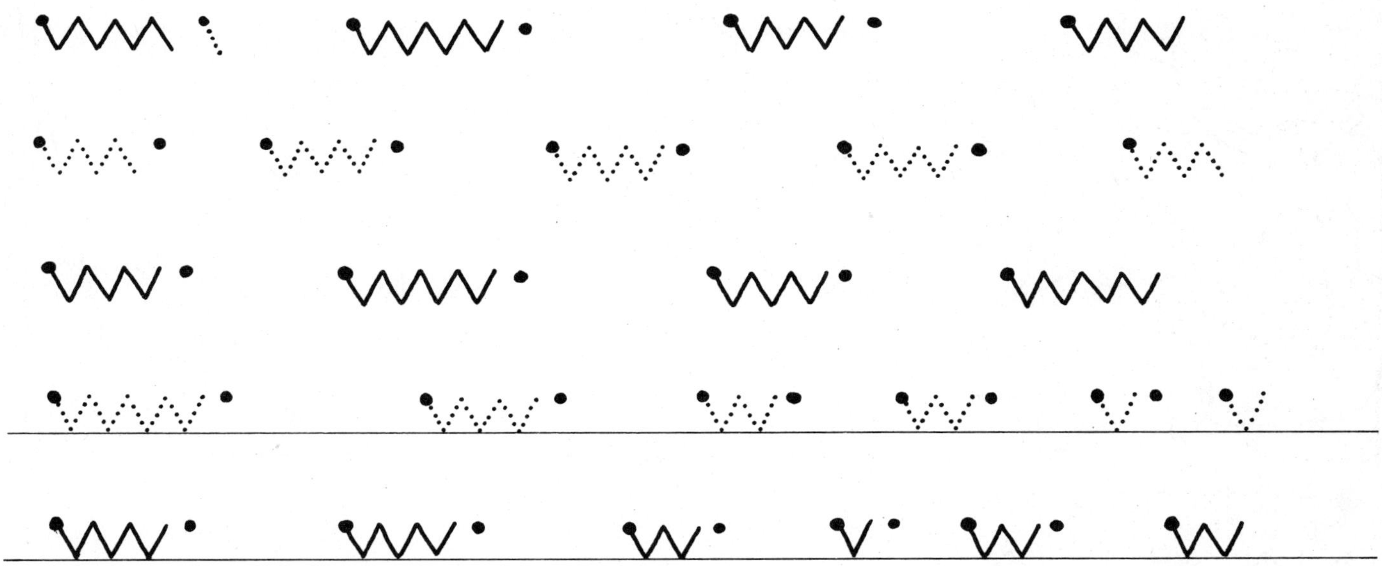

● Finish the line. V W V W ______________________________

● Finish the pattern on the dragon.

Name ______________________

- Finish the patterns round the suns.

- Finish the patterns on the crowns.

- Finish the patterns on the mats.

● Name ______________________

● Can you make the clothes look the same?

● **Name** ____________________

● Go over the pattern and copy in between. Remember – start at the dot!

● Finish the line.

● Finish the patterns on the balloons.

● Name ______________________

● Finish the patterns on the butterflies.

● Finish the patterns on the socks.

● Finish the patterns on the plates.

● Name ____________________

● Can you make the books and the hens look the same?

● **Name** ______________________

● Go over the pattern and copy in between. Remember – start at the dot!

Finish the line.

● Finish the pattern on the owl.

● **Name** ______________________________

● Finish the patterns on the tiles.

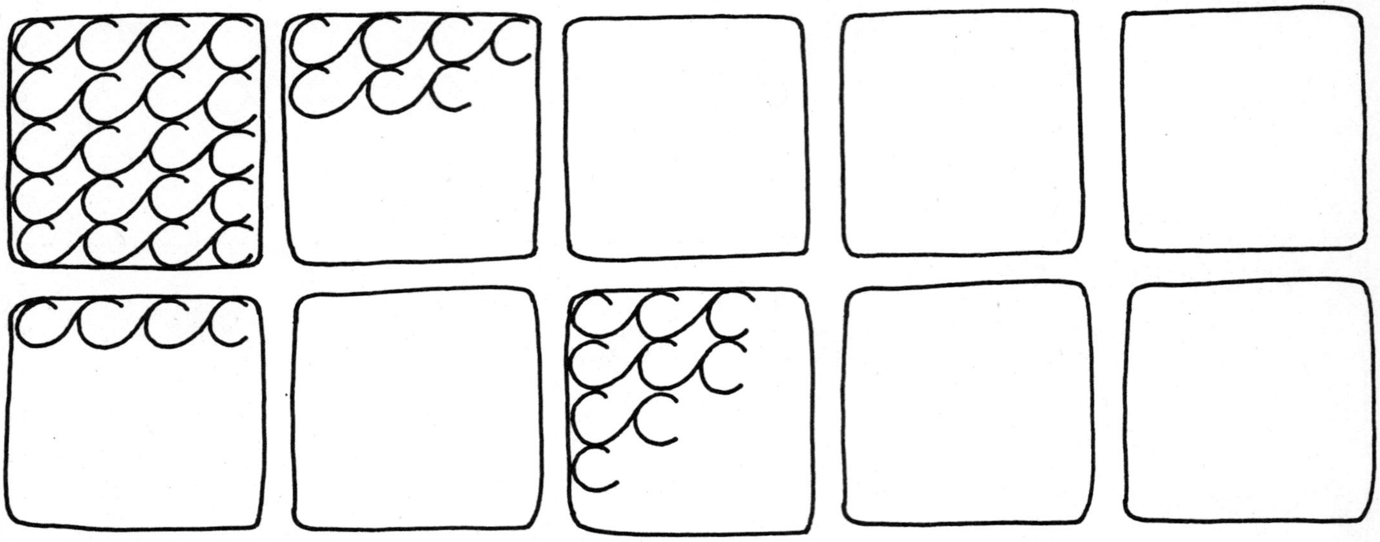

● Finish the patterns on the curtains.

● Finish the pattern on the carpet.

● Name ______________________

● Can you finish the wave patterns?

● Name ____________________

● Go over the pattern and copy in between.

● Now ask a friend to watch you complete the lines.

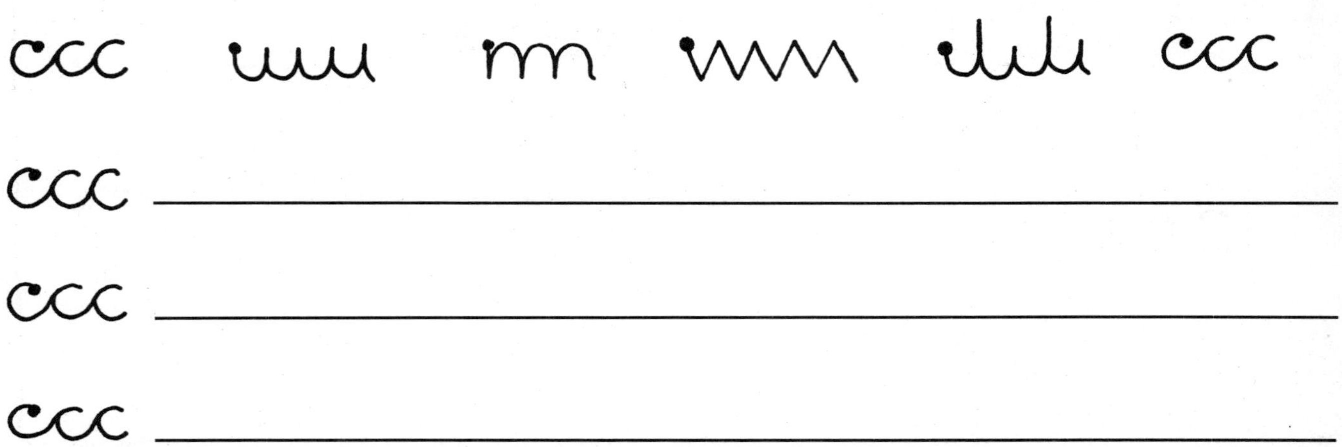

Name ______________________

- Finish each line.

- Now ask a friend to watch you complete the lines.
You choose the pattern.

● **Name** ______________________

● Can you make up some patterns? Here are some to help you.

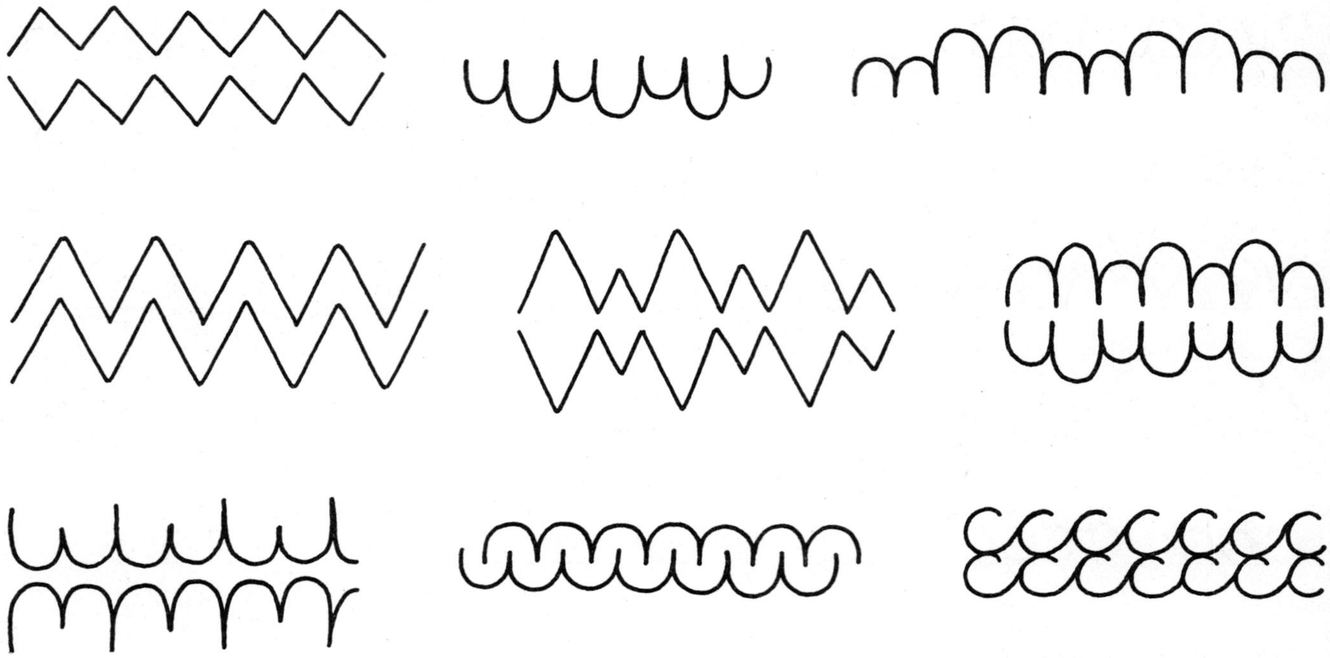

● Draw a pattern in the border.
Now draw a picture inside the border.

● Name ____________________________

● Finish the picture and the border. Make the lines and patterns go the same way. Don't use a ruler.

● **Name** ____________________________

● Finish the picture and the border. Make the lines and patterns go the same way.

● **Name** ______________________

● Finish the picture and the border. Make the lines and patterns go the same way. Don't use a ruler.

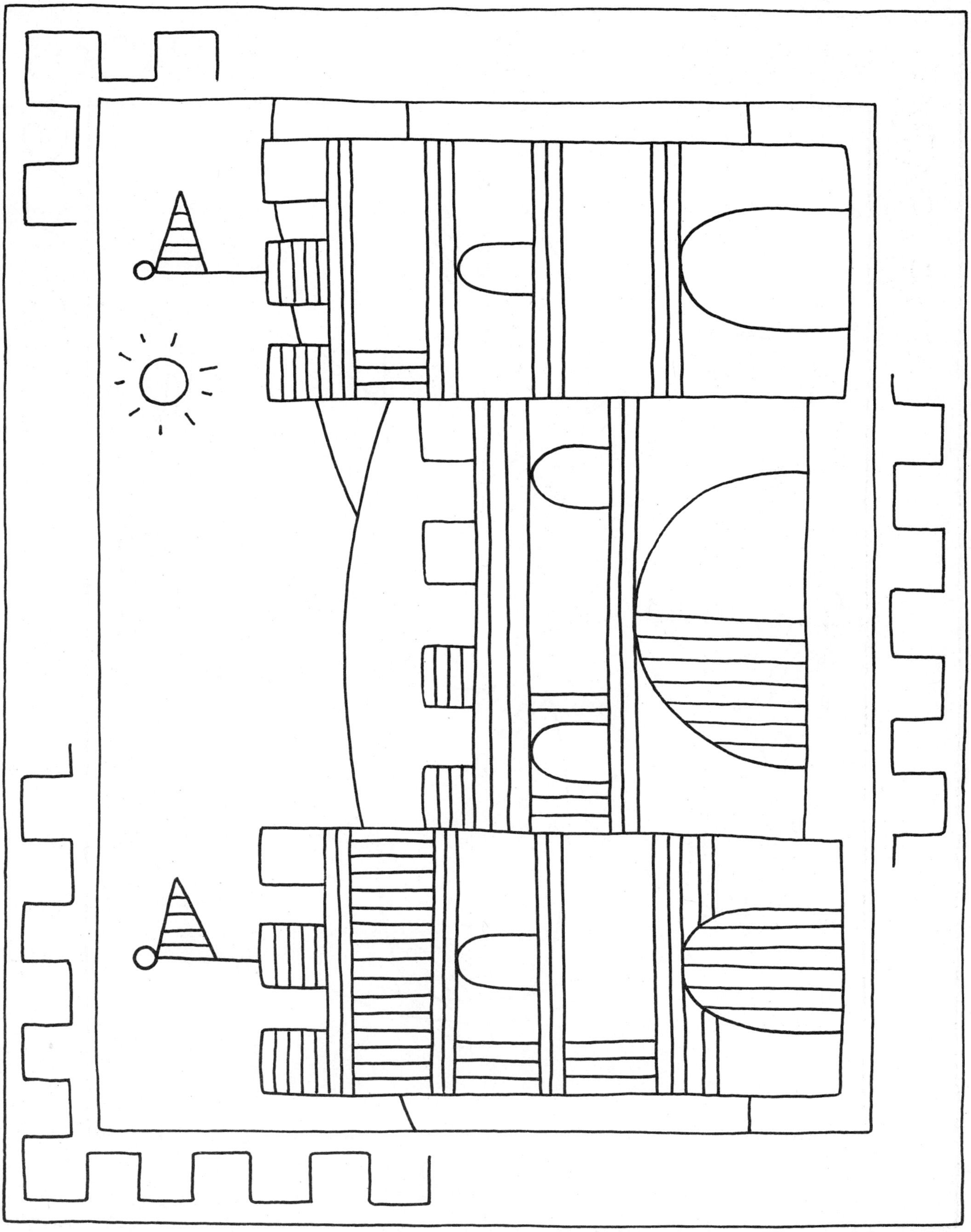

● **Name** ______________________________

● Finish the picture and the border. Make the lines and patterns go the same way. Don't use a ruler.

Name ______________________________

Finish the picture and the border. Make the lines and patterns go the same way. Don't use a ruler.

● **Name** ______________________________

● Finish the picture and the border. Make the lines and the patterns go the same way. Don't use a ruler.

● Name ____________________

Name ______________________